Scotti

Quotes, Jokes and Cartoons

Desi Northup
The Cartoon Guru

Made in the USA

Desno Publishing Co.
Route 3 Hopkinton NH 03229

Scottish fathers are men who give away their daughters to other men who aren't nearly good enough, so they can have grandchildren

who are smarter that everybody else's.

He that laughs at his ain joke

spoils the sport o' it.

How many Scotsman does it take to change a light bulb?

Och!

It's not that dark.

If it was not for the last minute, a lot of things in this house

would never get done.

What do you call
a Scottish dog lead?

McLeish.

Learn young, learn fair; learn old,

learn more.

A rich man's wooing need seldom

be a long one.

The difference between genius and

stupidity is that

genius has its limits.

A man is a lion

in his own cause.

There are three rules

to being a great father.

Patience, patience, patience.

Honesty is a trail. Once you get off it

you are lost.

"Come quickly doctor!
Sandy's just got dragged
under a tractor by his clothing."
"Kilt?"

"Not quite,
but he's badly injured."

Nane can play the fuil as weel as

a wise man.

Scotts love the summer.
For most of them,

it's their favorite day of the year.
McTavish went on a vacation to Canada. Sitting in a restaurant, he noticed a huge stuffed animal on the wall with large antlers.
He asked the waitress,
"What d'ye call that?"
"That – why that's just a moose," replied the waitress.
"Jings!" exclaimed McTavish. "I'd hate to see how big the cats are."

Father's day is always a worrying time

for Scottish dads.

Ma stomach

thinks ma throat is cut.

Everyone in this house is entitled

to my opinion.

"Did you enjoy yer vacation at Saltcoasts?"
"Aye."
"And did you have good weather?"
"Aye, but I missed it –

I was in the

bathroom at the time."

Excuses are like belly buttons –

useless.

He's the slave of all slaves who serve's

none but himself.

The one who quits last…

wins.

Two Scottish ducks were flying along. One turns and says, "Quack, quack."
The other turns around and says,

"A'm going as quack as I can."

The devil's boots

don't creak.

In Scotland there are only two seasons.

Winter and July.

Everybody gets knocked down.

Champs get back up.

Why do bagpipers walk
when they play?

To get away from the noise.

They that dance

must pay the fiddler.

What's a definition

of a gentleman?

Someone who knows how to play bagpipes.

but doesn't.

If you don't have time to do it right,

when will you have time to do it over?

How many Edinburghians does it take to change a light bulb?
Just one – to hold the light bulb and then expect the world

to revolve around him.

Even the langest day will

hae an end.

Life is like Rudolph the red-nosed reindeer. If you are no' in front then

the scenery never changes.

Death is death,

and will hear no denial.

Pay as you go, if you canna pay

dinna go.

A Scottish prayer – "Oh Lord, we do not ask you give us wealth.

But show us where it is."

If you are in deep water

keep your mouth shut.

Did you hear about the Scotsman who got caught making nuisance phone calls?

He kept reversing the charges.

The more mischief

the better sport.

Sign on a Scottish golf course:
"Members must refrain from picking up lost balls until

they have stopped rolling."

Don't find fault,

find the remedy.

Government cutbacks are really starting to affect Glasgow General Hospital. The only heart and lung machine left is the

haggis grinder in the kitchen.

Sudden friendship,

sure repentance.

A Scots pessimist is a man who feels badly when he feels good for the fear he'll feel worse

when he feels better.

Success is how high you bounce when

you hit the bottom.

Clipped sheep will

growe again.

OK. Be bad.

It will save Santa a trip.

He's as welcome as water in

a holed ship.

What do you call a Scottish parrot?

A macaw.

We can forgive the debt,

but not for unkindness.

Three Scotsmen have been murdered while wearing kilts. Police are beginning to see

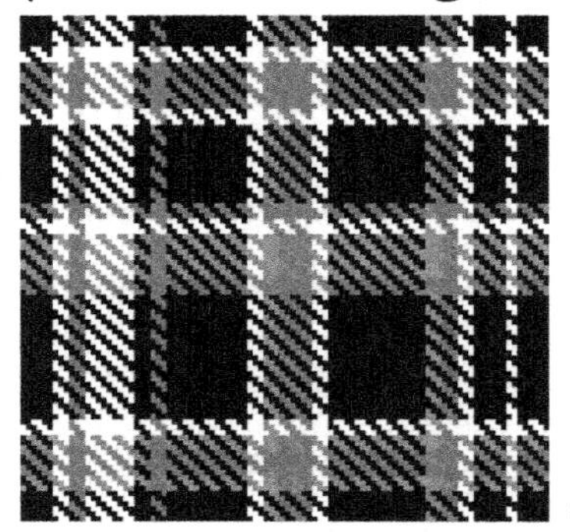

a pattern.

Secrets are only things

you give to others

to keep for you.

Did you hear about a man
who gave up making haggis?

He didn't have
the guts for it anymore.

When drink's in,

wit's oot.

With heavy snow on the way, Glasgow city council has been preparing by stockpiling salt. The chip shops must not be allowed

to run out again.

A bad wound may heal,
but a bad name will kill.

Two negatives make a positive but only in Scotland do two positives make a negative –

"Aye right."

Put your hand nae farther than your

sleeve will reach.

Don't wait for success, go ahead

without it.

Ye maunna tramp on

the Scots thistle.

Must is king's word.

It never rains,

but it pours.

I'm not a pessimist,

I'm just Scottish.

There is no right way to do

the wrong thing.

Resent historical research has revealed why Scotsmen wear kilts. In 1357 Angus McDougal won a lady's tartan skirt

in a raffle.

God sends meat an' the de'il

sends cooks.

Donald and his brother Sandy were running the ferry service. One day it was very stormy and the boat tossed about violently on the giant waves.

"We'll sink, we'll sink!"
 wailed Donald.

"Quick, then, collect the fares," shouted Sandy.

"Otherwise we will all be drooned afore they've paid."

A Scots mist will weet an Englishman

tae the skin.

How was copper wire invented?
Two Scotsmen were arguing

over a penny.

Ideas don't work

till you do.

While staying at a country hotel, McNab noticed with disappointment the tiny pots of honey on the breakfast table. When the landlady came into the room, McNab solemnly pointed to one and said,

"I see ye keep a bee."

Have you heard about the Scotsman who gave a present of fifty pounds each to an Englishman, an Irishman and a Welshman?

Nor has anyone else.

They that drink langest

live langest.

If mairages is made in hieven,

you twa has few friends there.

If opportunity doesn't knock,

build your own door.

Aim for the moon even if you only hit

the lamppost.

He that speaks the thing he should not, shall surely hear the thing

he would not.

Good enough is not

good enough.

If some folks would talk only when they think,

they'd hear a pin drop.

Half a tale is enough

for a wise man.

When poverty comes in at the door

friendship flees oot at the window.

The man at the top of the mountain

didn't fall there.

Penny wise and

pound foolish.

Don't marry for money,

you can borrow it cheaper.

He that lives upon hope

has a slim diet.

Remember.

A loaded gun beats four aces.

A wee moose can creep under a great corn stack.

Never give cherries to the pig or

advice to the fool.

He that gets, forgets, but he that

wants, thinks on.

Did you hear about the generous Scotsman who offered a million pounds to the first person to swim

non-stop across the Atlantic ocean?

Be happy while you're livin, for you're

a lang time deid.

He who finds no fault in himself

needs a second opinion.

Daring and doing beats

worrying and waiting.

Take a man by his word and a cow

by his horns.

When the cup is full,

carry it even.

Don't be afraid to give up good and

go for great.

A wise man carries his cloak in fair weather, an' a fool wants his

in the rain.

Confessed faults

are half mended.

A man that is warned

is hauf armed.

A hired horse

never tired.

Don't look where you fell,

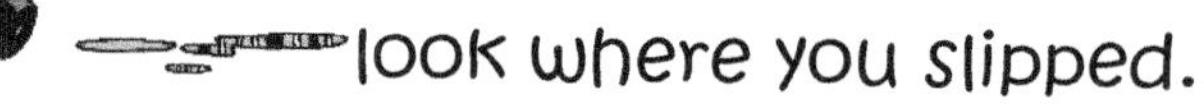

look where you slipped.

Experience

may teach fools.

If you don't see the bottom

don't wade.

You'll go stony-broke if you wait aroon

the hoose waitin' for a break.

A woman is best when
she is openly bad.

The more noble

the more humble.

Bees that has honey in their mooths

has stings in their tails.

Ye cannae plough the field jist by turnin' it ower

in yer mind.

There are thousands of folks out there happy to separate you

from your money.

Envy is the rack of the soul and the

torture of the body.

Every man's tale is guid till

anither's be tauld.

Folks may doubt what you say,

but they always believe what ye do.

The sooner you fall behind,

the more time

you have to catch up.

The devil's a busy bishop

in his own diocese.

Don't shake the tree over hard, you

never just know what might fall out.

What's yours is mine,

what's mines is my ain.

Ye needn't poor water on a drooned mouse.

Grin when ye win,

and laugh when ye lose.

Work like you don't need money;

love like you've never been jilted;

and dance like nobody's watching.

Better wade back mid watter than

gang forrit an droon.

If you don't want anyone to know,

don't do it.

You only eat an elephant

in wee bites.

Laws catch flies, but let hornets

go free.

Confession is gude

for the saul.

There's nae medicine

for fear.

Don't try to catch tow frogs

with one hand.

Better be deid

than oot o' fashion.

Children are natural mimics.

They act like their fathers in spite of all their mother's best efforts to teach them good manners.

When the hert is full

the tongue will speak.

He who hesitates

is probably right.

Better keep the devil at the door than

have to turn him

out of the house.

If ye're born to be hanged then

ye'll no' be drowned.

It's better to try and fail,

than fail to try.

Keep your tongue

within your teeth.

Opportunity knocks, but temptation just stands ootside the door

an' whistles.

How do you recognize a left-handed Scotsman?

He keeps all his money
in his right-hand pocket.

Necessity

has no laws.

Man's best candle is his

understanding.

A favorable wind does not

blow forever.

The trouble with getting wiser is that

you have to get older

at the same time.

Don't count the days,

make the days count.

He has licked

the butter of my bread.

If you afraid to go too far,

you will never go far enough.

Nobody listens until

you make a mistake.

Never underestimate the power of

human stupidity.

Watch it. Temptation always gives you

a second chance.

Ye should be king

o' your word.

Forbid a fool a thing

an' that he'll do.

Failure follows the path of least

resistance.

The day has sight,

the night has ears.

Things turn out best for people who make the best of the way

things turn out.

He has gotten a bite

on his ain bridle.

Why do all Scots have a sense of humor?

Because it's free.

A father's advice is like castor oil.
Easy to give,

but awful to take.

Dirt parts

good company.

If you are too big for your breeks,

you're exposed in the end.

If you think it's going well,

you've forgotten something.

He that peeks through a keyhole

may see what will vex him.

There is little ill said that is not

ill ta'en.

Put your finger in the fire an' say

it was your fortune.

To marry is to halve your rights and

double your duties.

Law-makers shou'd na be

paw-breakers.

There's the only way to improve memory.

Lend the family money.

By the time a man realizes that maybe his father was right, he usually has a son

who thinks he's wrong.

It's ok wi' me if it's ok

wi' yer mother.

Greatness never came from

not trying.

If God had wanted us tae touch oor toes,

he'd of stuck them oan oor knees.

Twelve highlanders and a bagpipe

make a rebellion.

The book o' maybes

is very braid.

It's no the burden, but the owerburden,

that kills the beast.

I'm sick an' tired o' the whole

jing-bang lot of ye.

Monday is a terrible way tae spend a

eventh o' yer life.

The only exercise you seem to get is

pushin' your luck.

It's the time when they go broke giving out money so their children can surprise them with the presents

they don't need.

If you don't believe in yourself,

nobody else will.

A young saint may prove

an old devil.

Egotism is an alphabet

of one letter.

If you think you can't, you won't.

If you think you can, you will.

A father was giving his son a lecture about lying.

"When I was your age I didn't tell lies."

"So how old were you when

you started, dad?"

He that teaches himself has a fuil for

his maister.

You cannot climb the ladder of success with your hands

in your pockets.

A child may have too much of

his mother's blessing.

Tourist: "I'm sorry, waiter, but I only have enough money for the bill. I have nothing left for a tip.
Highland waiter:

"Let me add up that bill again, sir."

A misty morning may be

a clear day.

He, who thinks by the inch and talks by the mile, deserves to be kicked by the foot.

Honesty has no pride.

If you always do what you have always done, then you will always get

what you have always got.

Ill herds makes

fat wolves.

What should not be heard by wee ears,

should not be said by big mouths.

He can lie as weel as a dog

can lick a dish.

Donald: "Have you ever seen one of those new machines that can tell when a person is telling a lie?"
Sandy: "Seen one?

I married one!"

Aw things hae an end,

but a loaf has twa.

This book *is another publication in the* ***Chromicals™*** *series; a trademark of Desno Publishing Co*

Chromicals ™

Description of an object, word, phrase or event presented and displayed in a manner with continually changing font sizes and styles, accompanied by an illustration that further defines that description of that subject, generally with a degree of comic relief.

You can find these and many other

BOOKS by DESI NORTHUP

either ON-LINE or at a BOOKSTORE Near you.